AMELIORATING NEGATIVE EMOTIONS

How to handle anger, anxiety and stress

Gio Bradley

Table of Contents

Chapter 1

Introduction to Anger

The emotions of stress and vigor are both present in anger. When we feel intimidated or when we believe we have been treated unfairly, this is a common reaction. Anger can occasionally be a highly acceptable and constructive emotion.

Anger, what is it?

However, there are other instances in which the environment, someone's gaze, or someone's words might cause this reaction. We may misread events, believing that we have been attacked or criticized in some way, which sets off the vicious cycle of being furious.

It can be quite difficult to break the habit of responding in this way, but we can learn to think and behave differently.

Adapting how we react to rage

Thoughts have a propensity to lend context to events or interpersonal encounters. You might think things like "it's unjust," "I've been treated unfairly," "they're incorrect," and "I'm being attacked."

The anger cycle can be followed by several emotions, including rage, irritation, anxiety, despair, shame, and guilt.

Adrenaline is released physically when we feel attacked. It gives the body energy and makes it more eager or prepared to handle the circumstance.

You may train your mind and body to think and behave differently by employing the next STOP approach.

Take a pause and halt now.

Watch yourself and ask, "What am I responding to?" What thoughts and feelings do I have?

Consider it from a distance and ask yourself, Is this a fact or an opinion? Am I interpreting things incorrectly? Do what is best for you or the circumstance and put what works into practice.

What is most beneficial? Ranting, rumination, and frustration. People frequently discuss feeling annoyed before becoming furious when they are angry.

Each of us occasionally feels the emotion of frustration. When your efforts to accomplish an objective are hampered, frustration results. It is the sensation we get when we anticipate something different from what actually occurs. It frequently happens when we have unrealistically high standards for ourselves or others.

Finding strategies to change the things we do or the thoughts we have when we are irritated can help us reduce the level of irritation we experience on a daily basis. When attempting to accept feelings of frustration, it has been shown that the following techniques are effective:

1. Understand the things that make you angry
2. Recognize your irrational expectations and assumptions.
3. Accept the difficulty you are experiencing, adhere to any problem-solving techniques, and create reasonable goals for yourself.
4. Effective and aggressive communication is key.

Venting

You can get your anger off your chest by venting. People frequently feel better right away after expressing their displeasure. However, other people report feeling guilty, humiliated, or depressed shortly after expressing their anger due to the harm they have caused another person.

Venting was once considered beneficial and good for easing anger issues. However, recent research revealed that expressing anger is unhealthy because it increases the likelihood of future anger.

Rumination

Rumination is the act of reflecting in depth on a subject. Rumination can sometimes be physically and emotionally damaging. People bring things (thoughts, memories, events) into their minds and chew on them repeatedly.

Rumination about one's anger may center on resentful recollections or ideas of injustice and retribution.

Studies have demonstrated that as part of the flight-or-fight response, cortisol and adrenaline levels rise during ruminative fury. However, these hormones remain in the blood if the person does not flee or fight, having an adverse effect on their immune system, sleep, and emotional health.

Heart disease and sadness have both been related to high amounts of these hormones. Additionally, there is evidence to support the idea that obsessing over earlier upsetting events may have a significant impact on the development of cardiovascular disease.

Finally, while getting angry frequently leads to issues, there are instances when it can be beneficial. Usually, there is a problem when the costs of anger outweigh the advantages of rage.

Chapter 2

How to handle Anxiety

Anxiety is characterized by thoughts of worry, fear, and apprehension that have an impact on one's thinking, feelings, and body.

People may feel out of control and have unpleasant thoughts as a result. Additionally, it may cause somatic symptoms including sweating, shaking, or shortness of breath.

Those who have been given an anxiety disorder diagnosis frequently experience these symptoms. They can, however, have an impact on anyone to diverse degrees at various times. Fortunately, there are practical methods you can employ to deal with worry both temporarily and permanently.

Pause, take a breath

Take a break whenever your anxiety attacks and consider what is causing you to feel uneasy. Typical anxiety symptoms include concern about a recent or distant event.

For instance, you can be concerned that something negative will occur in the future. It's possible that you're still furious about something that already happened. No matter what you are concerned about, a significant portion of the issue is that you are not paying attention to the present.

When you shift your attention away from your worries and back to the present, anxiety begins to dissolve.

The next time your nervousness starts to distract you from the moment, sit down and take a few deep breaths to reclaim your composure. You can regain a sense of balance and return to the present moment by pausing for a moment and taking a deep breath. If you have the time, consider advancing this practice by experimenting with a breathing technique and mantra.

Try doing these easy breathing exercises:

Put yourself in a relaxed sitting position.

Put your eyes closed and take a calm, deep breath. After taking a deep breath in, let it out through your nose.

Continue to inhale and exhale completely through your nose. Let your breathing serve as a beacon for the now.
As you breathe, repeat the phrase "Be present."

Think of the word "be" to yourself with each inhalation, and the word "present" with each exhalation.

Breathing exercises are effective relaxation strategies that can help you reduce anxiety while focusing on the here and now.

Determine what is bothering you.
You need to identify what's upsetting you in order to address the underlying cause of your anxiety. You can accomplish this by setting aside some time to examine your emotions and thoughts.

A fantastic method to connect with your sources of anxiety is journaling. Try keeping a journal or notepad next to your bed if you notice that your anxiety-related thoughts are keeping you awake at night. All the things that are bothering you should be put in writing. Another technique to identify and comprehend your nervous feelings is to talk to a friend.

Consider the Things You Can Change

Many times, anxiety is caused by worrying about events that may never happen or haven't even happened yet. For instance, even if everything is OK, you could still be concerned about prospective problems like losing your job, being sick, or ensuring the safety of your loved ones.

No matter how hard you try, life can be unpredictable, and you can't always control what happens. You can, however, choose how you will approach the unknowable. By letting go of fear and putting your attention on thankfulness, you can use your worry as a source of power.

Change your perspective on your fears to replace them. For instance, instead of worrying about your job security, consider how appreciative you are that you still have one. Make a commitment to giving your all at work. Spend time with them or show them your appreciation instead of worrying about their safety. You can develop a more optimistic mindset with some practice.

At times, a genuine situation in your life may be what's causing your anxiety. It may be reasonable for you to be concerned about losing your job in light of frequent company layoffs or talk of downsizing. Taking action in this circumstance can be the key to lowering your tension. You might need to start job seeking and update your resume, for instance.

Get distracted

Sometimes, it may be most beneficial to simply change your attention away from your fear. You might feel the need to help others, perform some housework, or indulge in a fun activity or hobby.

You might:

1. Perform some housework or a project.
2. Take part in an artistic endeavor, such as writing, painting, or drawing.
3. Take a stroll or indulge in another sort of physical activity.
4. Playing music
5. Pray or reflect
6. Watch a hilarious movie or read an excellent book.

Build Up Your Body and Mind

Changes in your way of life can also be beneficial for preventing anxiety and assisting you in coping with anxiety attacks. Your degree of physical activity, how much sleep you get, and what you eat can all affect how anxious you feel.

Mood and stress levels can be impacted by what you eat, according to research. For instance, those who consume diets high in fruits and vegetables typically have lower stress levels.

Regular physical activity has also been linked to benefits for reducing and preventing anxiety, according to research. According to one study, physical activity considerably lessens anxiety symptoms while also having a preventative impact against anxiety disorders.

Your mental health and anxiety levels can both be greatly impacted by sleep. One risk factor for anxiety disorders, including generalized anxiety disorder, according to research, is sleep issues. An increase in tension and anxiety can result from even brief sleep disturbances.

Chapter 3

Unknotting Cognitive Dissonance

When a person's action conflicts with their ideals or beliefs, they experience cognitive dissonance, which can be uncomfortable. It can also happen when a person simultaneously maintains two opposing views.

It is not a disease or illness to have cognitive dissonance. Anyone can experience this psychological condition. In the 1950s, American psychologist Leon Festinger created the idea.

Cognitive dissonance: What is it?

When a person has two connected but opposing cognitions, or thoughts, cognitive dissonance results. The idea was first proposed in 1957 by psychologist Leon Festinger.

Festinger argued that two concepts can be consonant or discordant in his work A Theory of Cognitive Dissonance. Dissonant concepts contradict one another while consonant ideas logically flow from one another.

A person might wear a mask in public if they want to protect other people and think the COVID-19 epidemic is real. This is harmony.

The same person's beliefs and actions would conflict if they accepted the COVID-19 pandemic as a reality while refusing to put on a mask. Dissonance exists here.

Uncomfort is caused by the dissonance between two opposing beliefs or between an idea and conduct. According to Festinger, cognitive dissonance is exacerbated when a person maintains numerous contradictory beliefs that are significant to them.

Cognitive dissonance symptoms

Since dissonance is a feeling a person has inside, it cannot be observed. As a result, it is impossible to identify cognitive dissonance from a person's behavior alone.

Festinger thought that due to the discomfort cognitive dissonance generates, everyone is motivated to avoid or fix it. When forced to deal with it, this can lead people to adopt specific protective mechanisms.

These defense mechanisms can be divided into three groups:

- Avoiding: In this, the dissonance is either avoided or ignored. A person may try to avoid events or persons who bring it up, dissuade others from talking about it, or divert their attention to time-consuming activities.

- Delegitimizing entails discrediting the dissonance supporting documentation. One way to achieve this is to disparage the individual, team, or circumstance that brought the dissonance to light. For instance, they can assert that it is biased or unreliable.

- Impact reduction: This entails downplaying the significance of cognitive dissonance in order to lessen its unpleasantness. In order to persuade themselves or others that the behavior is acceptable, a person may do this by asserting that the behavior is unusual or an isolated incident.

Alternatively, people could strive to fix the contradiction by taking action. Cognitive dissonance can be overcome by either altering one's conduct or one's beliefs to make them more compatible with one another.

Cognitive dissonance examples

The following are some instances of cognitive dissonance:

Smoking: Despite knowing that smoking is bad for their health, many people nevertheless smoke. People who place a high priority on their health will experience dissonance to a greater extent.

Consuming meat: Some people who consider themselves to be animal lovers do consume meat, yet they may experience discomfort when they consider the source of their meat. This is regarded as the "meat conundrum" by some academics.

Household duties: A man may consciously or unconsciously expect his female partner to handle the majority of the household tasks or child rearing despite believing in the equality of the sexes.

Supporting fast fashion: Despite being aware of the negative consequences that fast fashion has on the environment and employees, some people continue to buy inexpensive clothing from businesses that use questionable business practices.

Cognitive dissonance's root causes

Cognitive dissonance can happen to everyone and is occasionally inevitable. People can't always act in a way that is consistent with their values.

The following are some elements that may lead to cognitive dissonance:

Forced compliance: A person may be required to do things they object to do their duties, refrain from harassment or abuse, or abide by the law.

Everyone just has a few options when making decisions. Cognitive dissonance may occur when a person must choose between multiple options they do not like or agree with, or when there is only one practical choice.

Effort: Even if something goes against a person's values, they tend to appreciate it highly when they have worked hard for it. This might be because it would be more dissonant to regard something badly after putting a lot of effort into it. Therefore, even if they disagree with the assignments morally, people are more inclined to perceive tough tasks positively.

Addiction is another element that might lead to cognitive dissonance. Even if a person may not wish to act in a contradictory way, addiction can make it feel physically and intellectually challenging to change one's conduct to conform to one's moral principles.

Cognitive dissonance's effects

People can be impacted by cognitive dissonance in a variety of ways. The pain of the dissonance itself or the coping strategies a person uses to deal with it may be related to the effects.

Stress or unhappiness may be exacerbated by the discomfort and tension cognitive dissonance causes within. Those who encounter dissonance yet are unable to overcome it could also feel helpless or guilty.

A person may fail to recognize their conduct and, as a result, fail to take action to overcome the cognitive dissonance if they avoid, delegitimize, or reduce the effects of the dissonance. This could injure them or others in various situations.

But cognitive dissonance can also be a tool for both individual and collective transformation. Bringing someone's attention to the tension between their actions and their principles may make them more conscious of the discrepancy and motivate them to take action.

For instance, a 2019 study mentions that therapies focused on dissonance may be beneficial for persons with eating problems. This method works by encouraging patients to speak out against their views on food and body image or to act in ways that do so. Dissonance results from this.

According to the theory behind this strategy, a person's implicit views about their body and thinness will alter to reconcile the dissonance, decreasing their urge to restrict their food intake.

According to the study, this intervention was successful for heterosexual women but less successful for nonheterosexual women for unknown reasons.

Overcoming Cognitive Dissonance

Ensuring that one's actions or values are compatible with each other is the best strategy to overcome cognitive dissonance.

One can accomplish this by:

Changing their behavior to reflect their beliefs entails changing one's activities. Compromises could be made in situations where a complete shift is not feasible. If a person who cares about the environment yet works for a polluting corporation cannot leave their employment, they might push for change at work.

Changing their beliefs: If someone constantly acts in a way that goes against their beliefs, they may start to doubt the significance of that belief or realize that they no longer hold it. Alternatively, they could introduce new ideas that better align their behavior with their beliefs.

A person may alter how they see the activity if they are unable or unwilling to alter the ideas or conduct that is the source of dissonance. For instance, a person who cannot afford to purchase from sustainable companies may be able to accept responsibility for their actions and recognize that they are doing what they can.

Seeking Assistance

A person does not always need treatment for cognitive dissonance because it is not a mental health problem. A person might seek treatment from a doctor or therapist if they find it difficult to stop a behavior or thought pattern that is upsetting them.

One might want to think about this if:
- They are addicted.
- They experience tension, anxiety, or low mood, and they feel intense guilt or shame over their behavior, which causes issues at work, in school, or their relationships.

When a person's conduct and beliefs conflict, they experience cognitive dissonance. This can also happen when they possess two opposing opinions. People try to feel better because it makes them feel uncomfortable.

Defense mechanisms like avoidance may be used by people to do this. Instead, by being conscious of their ideals and actively seeking opportunities to live those beliefs, people may lessen cognitive dissonance.

When feeling defensive or dissatisfied, a person may wonder what part cognitive dissonance may have had in their feelings.

People may gain from chatting with a therapist if they are a component of a larger issue that is upsetting them.

Chapter 4

Emotional stability

Everyone is susceptible to some level of emotional stress as life continues to function despite the present worldwide epidemic, which is unlike anything most of us have ever experienced. Everything we do is centered on our emotions. gaining control over your ideas, choices, and actions. Ever-rising insecurity breeds ever-rising anxiety, which can send our emotions flying all over the place. Therefore, maintaining mental stability is crucial during this pandemic.

Emotional stability: what is it?

The capacity to maintain emotional balance and stability is referred to as emotional stability. Being emotionally stable entails being able to maintain composure under pressure and having a limited range of unpleasant emotions. As a result, you are more prepared to handle whatever life throws at you while still being effective and capable.

Your emotions have unmatched power because, as was already established, they affect your actions, thoughts, and choices. You might, for instance, pass your driving test. You feel incredibly happy and excited as a result. Your feelings make things look so much better, giving you a fresh sense of freedom to roam. You decide to go out and celebrate with your pals since you just passed your driving test and are feeling so joyful.

Positive and negative emotions both have an impact on us; they are not mutually exclusive. People frequently experience the emotions of anger, fear, resentment, annoyance, and worry. These unfavorable feelings can increase stress and affect your decisions, actions, and thoughts.

Why is emotional balance crucial?

Self-confidence Criticism is an essential aspect of life since it shows us that nobody is perfect and that we can all improve. Nevertheless, it is impossible to avoid feeling hurt or deflated when we receive it.

Despite the disappointment, you will continue to pursue your goals if you are emotionally stable because you will feel more at ease in your skin.

Focus

A curveball can always happen in daily life; just take a look at the current pandemic, which no one predicted and which has devastated a lot of people. Anxiety and terror can overtake you during these times.

Those with great emotional stability will remain focused even during challenging and trying times. ensuring that they maintain

control and restrain their emotions.
allowing you to remain productive and
focused despite the difficulties to find a
solution.

Positivity

Nobody likes being forced out of their
comfort zone; when this happens, people
frequently feel anxious or afraid. You also
frequently lack self-assurance or start to
doubt your abilities. These feelings tend to
bring out the worst in individuals.

Those who are emotionally stable can see
the end of the tunnel and stop those
negative feelings and thoughts from gaining
. By keeping a positive attitude, trusting that
whatever is happening will pass, and staying
upbeat, you can overcome the current
obstacle.

Assessment

One of the traits that can be challenging to evaluate without a psychometric evaluation is emotional stability. In addition to covering emotional stability, a good personality test will also include the subscales necessary to conduct a thorough study of this feature in candidates.

We all confront problems in life; some of them we may anticipate, but others always take us off guard. When circumstances like these arise, emotional stability shines.

www.ingramcontent.com/pod-product-compliance
Lightning Source LLC
Chambersburg PA
CBHW071241140726
47996CB00007B/2698